CAL[illegible] FOOTPRINT

To Josephine,
Always follow
your dreams!
Sarah Sweeney
15-11-2015

Written and illustrated by
Sarah Sweeney

kidz
REDHOUSE KIDZ
ÇOCUK KİTAPLARI

SEV Yayıncılık Eğitim ve Ticaret A.Ş.
Nuhkuyusu Cad., No. 197 Üsküdar İş Merkezi, Kat 3,
34664 Bağlarbaşı, Üsküdar, İstanbul
Tel.: (0216) 474 23 43 • Sertifika No. 12603

Redhouse Reading Set, Calum's Footprint

Yazan ve Resimleyen: Sarah Sweeney
Yayın Yönetmeni: Ebru Şenol
Editör: Burcu Ünsal
Kapak ve İç Tasarım: Hüseyin Vatan

Birinci Baskı: Eylül 2015

ISBN: 978-605-9781-05-3

REDHOUSE SEV YAYINCILIK

Kütüphane Bilgi Kartı (CIP):
Sweeney, Sarah
Redhouse Reading Set, Calum's Footprint
1. Çocuk Edebiyatı 2. Yabancı Dil Eğitimi 3. İngilizce
İstanbul, SEV Yayıncılık, 2015, 68 Sayfa
ISBN: 978-605-9781-05-3

Baskı: A4 Ofset Matbaacılık San. ve Ticaret Ltd. Şti.
Yeşilce Mah., Donanma Sok., No. 16 Oto Sanayi Sitesi, 34418,
Kâğıthane, İstanbul
Tel.: (0212) 281 64 48 • Sertifika No. 12168

BEFORE YOU READ

1. Have you ever had an exciting dream that you wish you could experience in real life? What was your dream about?

2. What do you know about dinosaurs? When did they live? What did they look like?

DON'T FORGET: There is a glossary on the last pages of this book where you can look up the meanings of the words you don't know.

INTRODUCTION

Calum had a magic bed. He told his friends at school about the bed once when he was younger, but they laughed at him so he didn't speak about it again. They already laughed at him because once the teacher said his name wrong and his classmates thought it was funny. After that he always reminded everyone that his name was pronounced 'kay-lum'. He didn't want the kids to have something else to laugh and tease him about.

That was long ago. Now he was older and no one giggled at his name anymore. But he still didn't talk to anyone about his magic bed. It was his *little* secret.

He didn't know why his bed was different from the other beds in his house or even where it came from. He vaguely remembered that his parents bought it at a department store when he was little. He had wanted a racecar bed, but they had assured him that when he was older he would like this bed more. They were right. It seemed like a normal bed when they bought it and brought it home many years ago. But the first night he slept in it was when he knew it was special. It was magic.

CHAPTER ONE

Almost every evening was the same. First, he had dinner with his mom, his dad and little brother Liam. Tonight they had spaghetti with meatballs. His brother liked making slurping noises with the noodles and usually made a mess. Calum loved spaghetti and liked to melt cheese all over it. It had always been one of his favorite meals.

After dinner he had to do his homework. Every year it was getting harder. That night he had social studies homework. Their teacher was teaching them how the earth looked 300 million years ago. He was amazed that all the pieces of land used to be connected so long ago. He answered some questions in his workbook and then put his books back in his bag. He liked to be organized for school in the morning.

When his homework was finished, Calum usually played with Liam for a little while. Sometimes they read books. Other times they did puzzles. Calum never got bored playing with his little brother and really liked to spend time with him.

Liam went to bed before Calum. Every night was the same. Liam always complained and asked "Can I stay up a little longer?" but their mom always shook her head and told him he had to go to sleep.

Calum never complained. He would brush his teeth and kiss his parents good night. Then he would quickly go to bed. His parents thought they were lucky that he never complained about having to go to bed, especially when he was a little boy.

"Good night," said his mom from the doorway as Calum crawled into bed.

DINOSAURS

"Good night," said his dad. "Sweet dreams!" It was a little joke between him and his father. When Calum was a little boy, he had told his dad about the magic bed and his father told him he just had really vivid dreams. He said he wished he had dreams like Calum because all he ever dreamed about was being in the office, filling out paperwork. Calum tried to convince him that the bed really was magic and that it wasn't just a dream, but his dad never believed him. Ever since then, his dad always wished him sweet dreams every night.

Calum pulled the covers up around him and snuggled into his bed. The bed was nice and warm. It had been a long day and he was tired. Calum knew it would be easy to sleep but he also knew he wouldn't sleep at all.

His parents closed his door and Calum listened as the sound of their footsteps became quieter and quieter as they walked down the hall, away from his room. He heard them turn the television

CALUM

back on and he could hear the nightly news. He could also hear the family cat, Daisy, who had sneaked into his room and curled into a ball and started sleeping at the end of the bed.

Calum closed his eyes and concentrated on his magic bed. Suddenly he felt a cool breeze blow across his face and he opened his eyes to see where he was. The bed was flying through the night sky!

CHAPTER TWO

He could see buildings below him. Their windows were dark. Everyone was sleeping. Daisy, at the end of the bed, got up and stretched. "Come here Daisy," Calum called to the cat. He was afraid she might fall off the bed. When she realized that the bed was moving, she quickly moved up to him and crawled under the covers, safely next to him. Since the cat liked to sleep on Calum's bed, it wasn't her first adventure on the magic bed with him.

Calum was a little nervous. He didn't like to say he was scared, but he worried a big wind might blow them both off the bed. He held on tight and closed his eyes, hoping that when he opened his eyes again they would be someplace exciting.

After a couple of minutes there was a thump as the bed landed on the ground. Calum felt warmth on his face and he slowly opened his eyes. The sun

was shining bright. Wherever the bed had taken him, it was morning and it was very noisy. Most of the noises were birds singing and chirping, but there were other animal sounds, too. It reminded him of the last time he was at the zoo with Liam. The animals sounded excited, like it was feeding time or something.

He looked around. They seemed to be in a forest. There were trees all around him. The sky was blue and the sun was already hot on his face. Calum tugged at the collar of his shirt. He was starting to sweat.

"Are you ready for an adventure Daisy?" he asked the cat. She meowed at him and went back to sleep. She wasn't an adventurous cat. She usually slept on the bed, wherever it took them.

Calum got out of the bed and started to explore. "*Where am I?*" he wondered. The ground was wet and he didn't really want to get his socks dirty. Otherwise his mother would ask questions and then she would think he was crazy when he gave her the right answers. He always had this problem when the bed took him somewhere dirty. Once he tried to think ahead and he actually put a pair of shoes at the foot of the bed, but his mother saw them and told him not to have shoes in the bed because they were dirty. After that, he didn't bring anything for his feet.

He found some big round rocks and leaned against them to take off his socks. But when he touched them, he realized they weren't rocks. "These are eggs!" he exclaimed forgetting to take off his socks. Huge eggs! He wondered what kind of animal could lay such big eggs. "*Maybe they are from an ostrich*," he thought. He heard that ostrich eggs were big, but he didn't think they would be that big. He hoped the mother of the eggs wasn't around.

The forest became very noisy all of a sudden. The leaves started rustling and moving a lot, but there was no wind. Something was coming but it was still far away. He glanced at the cat who was

still in the bed. She heard the noise too; her ears were back, so she was listening carefully.

The noise was quickly getting louder and louder, which meant that whatever was making the noise was coming closer. It also meant that whatever it was, it was very big.

Suddenly, the cat jumped off the bed and ran away from Calum into the forest.

"Daisy!" Calum shouted after the cat, but she was gone.

Calum turned and looked back at the forest, just in time to see the mother of those eggs. But it was not an ostrich. It was a huge dinosaur! The magic bed had taken him back in time!

CHAPTER THREE

"Daisy! Wait for me!" he shouted, running after the little cat.

The dinosaur sniffed her eggs. Satisfied that they weren't hurt, she turned in Calum's direction and roared the loudest roar he had ever heard, and then started to run after him. Calum

had been interested in dinosaurs when he was a little boy, but he didn't remember very much about them now. He was surprised by how loud the roar was. Calum didn't stop to think about it though, he kept running. He wasn't sure where he was going. He just knew he had to find the cat and get away from the angry dinosaur.

After a while, Calum's legs started to get tired. He felt like he had been running for hours, but he knew it probably wasn't that long. It was hard to run because he kept slipping and his feet kept getting stuck in the mud. There was no noise behind him anymore and the forest was quiet again. He was sure the dinosaur had stopped chasing him.

The forest seemed less like the forests he knew back home and it was more like a jungle. The trees had big leaves and in some places there were so many trees that he couldn't even see the sky through their leaves. There were strange and beautiful plants all around him, some with colorful flowers. "*This must be what a jungle is like,*" thought Calum, who had only seen jungles on TV or on the Internet.

He looked around for a place to sit and found some more rocks. Calum inspected them carefully, but they were real rocks this time. He wiped the sweat off his forehead. It was very hot out here. He looked at his feet. His socks were covered in mud and so were his pants. "*Mom's going to be really angry at me*," he thought, "*but she will be angrier if I don't find Daisy*."

Calum took a deep breath and got off the rocks. He had to find that cat.

Even though he had read books about dinosaurs when he was younger, he didn't know what to do if he came across one. He heard once that if you met a bear you should fall to the ground and pretend you were dead, but he didn't think it would work with a dinosaur. He thought the dinosaur would just assume he was an easy meal and eat him up. He didn't want to admit that he was scared but he was beginning to worry. Then he remembered what his dad told him when he was a little boy.

"You can be scared for five seconds," his dad had said. "After five seconds, you need to be brave."

Calum thought his dad's wisdom was useful now. He took a deep breath. Even though he felt silly, he counted, "One... Two... Three... Four... Five." It seemed to work. He felt a little braver. "DAISY!" he shouted loudly and started walking again.

Calum saw different dinosaurs while he searched for the cat. He tried to remember the different names of dinosaurs that he knew, but he could only remember Triceratops and Tyrannosaurus rex. He remembered that the T-Rex was a

1, 2, 3, 4, 5

meat-eater and he was sure Triceratops could be dangerous too but luckily, he saw neither of them. He also saw animals that he didn't think were dinosaurs but they didn't look like any animals he'd ever seen before. A lot of the birds looked different too. Even a few mice scurried past him, but they didn't look like the mice his mother was scared of either. They were much bigger!

Most of the dinosaurs that he saw were so big that they didn't even notice him on the ground next to their feet. They just walked right past him. Some dinosaurs occasionally stopped to sniff him, but they weren't interested in his smell and moved on.

He called for Daisy again and again. "Daisy! Where are you? Here kitty kitty..." He wished he had some fishy treats or something to get her to come. When they were home the cat always came if his mother called for her, but that was because his mom was the one who fed her. She never came for anyone else. Calum's dad always joked that she wasn't a dog.

Then he heard a noise coming from up in a tree above him. He looked up hoping to see his little cat. But it wasn't the cat.

CHAPTER FOUR

Two beady brown eyes stared back at Calum from the tree. A little face emerged from behind the leaves. It almost looked like a child's face, but it was completely covered in brown fur, with big round furry ears. It was a monkey! The monkey made some weird noises and squealed at Calum. But it didn't scare him.

He knew the monkey wouldn't understand him but he tried speaking to it anyway. "I'm lost," he said to the little face staring down at him. "And my cat is lost too. I really need to find her before a dinosaur eats her or something."

The monkey stared at him for a minute and

then swung from the tree, landing on Calum's shoulder. Calum was surprised when the monkey stayed on his shoulder and seemed to make itself comfortable.

Then the little monkey tapped Calum on the head and pointed ahead in the distance. Maybe the monkey knew where to go.

Calum was starting to get more comfortable in this world of dinosaurs and he wasn't scared of them as before. Even though he knew the little monkey couldn't keep him safe from a dinosaur, it did help just to have a new little friend. But he knew he couldn't stay in this world for too long though. It would soon be morning and his family would be looking for him (and his bed and the cat).

"Maybe Daisy is smart enough to go back to the bed," he thought to himself. "We need to find the bed again," he said to the monkey. But the monkey was only interested in eating the fruit he found. Calum was starting to get hungry, so he

tried one of the berries that the monkey was eating, but it was so sour he had to spit it out.

"We should find something tasty to eat. That's disgusting!" he told the monkey.

Suddenly the monkey jumped off his shoulder and ran into the forest.

"Monkey! Monkey!" Calum called after the animal. But it was gone. Now he was alone again.

"I have to do this," he said out loud. "I have to do this on my own. No one will help me. Certainly not a monkey..."

He turned around, thinking it would be best to walk back the way he had come, but nothing looked familiar anymore. This time he really was lost. He felt helpless. All he wanted was to find the cat and go back home. He had had enough of this dinosaur world.

"One... Two... Three... Four... Five..." he counted again and continued on his journey. He wondered how many times he would have to count to five before leaving this nightmare of an adventure.

He heard something growling. It sounded very close. He looked around, but he was alone. He laughed when he realized it was his stomach growling. He was getting really hungry! *"If only I had eaten more of the monkey's sour berries,"* he thought.

While looking for something to eat, he heard a scratching and chirping noise in the trees. He looked up, hopeful that the monkey might have come back. All of a sudden, something hit his head and fell on the ground.

It was a banana!

CHAPTER FIVE

"A banana!" shouted Calum. He knew he wasn't going to starve since he had eaten two plates of spaghetti for dinner just a couple of hours ago, but he was really hungry after all that running around. He picked up the banana and then looked up at the tree. The runaway little monkey was looking down at him, chirping loudly.

Something was making noise in the forest behind them. He heard a loud growl, but this time he knew it wasn't coming from his stomach. Calum felt sure it was another dinosaur!

The monkey pointed into the forest, away from the noise and disappeared into the trees again.

Calum started running too, following the monkey. Anywhere away in the forest would be better than being in the path of an angry dinosaur.

In some places the forest was clear and it was easy to run, but in other places there were lots of branches and leaves making it hard to move. Calum came across another nest of dinosaur eggs, but he was careful not to break any of them. The mother of these eggs just roared at him, but she didn't chase him like the other dinosaur had.

He ran through mud puddles that were so deep he sank into the mud and almost had to crawl out. The mud was warm from the sun and went up his pants all the way to his knees. In one puddle his foot got stuck. The mud was getting extra sticky as it started to dry in the sun. He struggled to pull his foot out. When it finally popped out of the mud, he saw that his foot was bare and his

sock was somewhere in the mud. He didn't care; he just had to get away from whatever was chasing him. He could still hear the roaring of the dinosaur following him. It sounded like it was getting closer.

He saw the little monkey in the distance and ran straight for it. There were fewer trees in the forest now, and the ground was drier, so it was easier for him to run. The monkey was standing on the ground in front of what looked like a

little entrance to a dark cave. He caught up to the monkey and followed it into the cave.

The cave entrance wasn't very big and Calum had to bend down to be able to get inside. After the brightness of the sun outside the cave, Calum felt completely blinded by the darkness inside. He hoped whatever dinosaur was chasing them would be too big to fit into the opening of the cave.

He crossed his fingers and just as he had hoped, the dinosaur was too big to get in. But that didn't stop it from trying to squeeze its head into the opening and roaring loudly. When Calum saw the dinosaur's head filling the entrance, he held his breath. It was a Tyrannosaurus rex! Suddenly it occurred to him that he had just outrun the most feared dinosaur ever, but now here it was staring at him with small angry eyes. When it couldn't get into the cave any further, the dinosaur's face blocked all the light. It was less than a couple of meters away from Calum. It was so close that when the dinosaur roared, its spit hit Calum's face.

He couldn't control himself anymore. No counting to five could make him brave with a T-Rex about to eat him. He closed his eyes tightly and screamed.

CHAPTER SIX

He screamed and screamed. For some reason, screaming seemed to help and after less than a minute he started to feel better. Then suddenly he felt light on his face. He wondered if it all really was a dream like his father always told him. He wondered if he would be at home in his bed when he opened his eyes. He hoped his father was right.

He opened his eyes slowly and looked around. He was still in the cave, but the Tyrannosaurus rex was gone and the entrance to the cave was clear. He heard a loud roar in the distance that sounded very much like the dinosaur that had roared at him only a moment before. He could also hear the normal forest sounds that he had begun to get used to.

Calum's eyes were starting to adjust to the darkness of the cave. He could almost make out the little monkey curled up and shaking next to him. The dinosaur had scared it too. He reached down carefully to pet its fur and try to calm it down. But as soon as his fingers touched it, the monkey opened its little mouth and bit his hand.

"Hey!" shouted Calum, pulling his hand away from the little animal. "What was that for?" But he knew even though the monkey seemed friendly, it probably had never seen a human

before and it was normal that it would bite him. Even Daisy bit him sometimes, but she mostly tried to bite Liam when he played too rough.

He stood up in the cave and looked around. There didn't seem to be anything interesting inside it. It wasn't like the caves you see in movies with a pile of bones in the corner or caveman artwork on the wall. It was just a boring cave.

"Do you think we can go out now?" he asked the little monkey.

The monkey was licking its paws and grooming itself. It looked up at Calum, chirped a bit and then slowly walked to the cave entrance.

Calum was really surprised by how much it acted like a little child. It paused at the entrance and carefully poked its head out. It looked to the left, then to the right, and then up into the trees. When the monkey was sure the dinosaur was gone, it stepped out into the sunshine. Calum followed it.

They walked around the side of the cave, and were surprised to see that just beyond the cave, the forest opened to a familiar little clearing and Calum saw his bed lying under the sun. He thought he had never seen such a beautiful sight. Everything looked just as he had left it.

As he got closer, he noticed a little lump under the blanket on his bed. He worried there might be a little dinosaur underneath. Even though he hadn't met any little dinosaurs, he had seen enough movies to know that the little dinosaurs could be just as dangerous as the big ones.

Calum hesitated for only a couple of seconds and then he carefully pulled back the blanket.

CHAPTER SEVEN

"Meow?" meowed his little cat, staring up at him. Her eyes were big and she seemed happy to see him.

"Daisy!" he shouted. The little monkey jumped to a tree just as Calum scooped the cat up into his arms. He was so relieved that it was his cat. He thought he might never see the cat again.

"I think it's time to go home kitty!"

She mewed again.

He jumped onto the bed. The cat had already started to purr against his neck. She was ready to go home too.

Suddenly the little monkey started squealing

loudly from the tree. Calum heard the noise at the same time as the monkey did. The Tyrannosaurus rex was back! The trees rustled as it moved quickly through the forest. The dinosaur's roar seemed angrier than before.

"Oh no!" shouted Calum. He quickly pulled the blankets up over himself and the cat. He looked up to the tree where the monkey was jumping around, chirping excitedly. "Thank you monkey!" Calum called to the monkey, even though he knew it couldn't possibly understand him. He was starting to think that maybe it did understand him a bit.

"Go! Hide!"

The monkey made one last noise and then disappeared into the forest again.

Calum hugged Daisy in his arms. "Let's go home," he said.

Calum shut his eyes tightly just as he heard the dinosaur roar. It was right next to the bed. Calum could smell its hot, bad breath on his face and feel its spit spray against his skin. He didn't dare to open his eyes. He only concentrated on going back home.

Suddenly, he felt the bed begin to move. He counted slowly, "One... Two... Three... Four... Five."

CHAPTER EIGHT

When Calum opened his eyes, he was back in his bedroom. Daisy was still in his arms under the covers. Daylight was shining through his bedroom curtains. It was morning.

He heard his mom walking down the hall. She opened his door and said, “Good morning sunshine! Sleep well?”

Calum sat up in the bed. The cat jumped up and ran out of his room. Calum didn’t want to sound silly but he couldn’t stop himself from telling his mother about the dinosaurs. When he finished his story, she laughed and said, “Sweetheart, it was just a dream. Your bed isn’t magic. See?” She sat on the bed, and closed her eyes. Nothing happened. "Calum, you're too old for this nonsense. Enough of this 'magic bed' talk, OK?"

Calum smiled. It was easier to just agree with her. "OK mom. Maybe you're right." She left him alone, so he could get dressed and come down for breakfast.

He glanced under the blankets. His feet and pants were covered in mud and one of his socks was missing.

Calum stayed a lot longer than usual in the bathroom that morning. It was harder to wash the mud out of his pants than he had expected. When he finally joined his family, his father was already sitting at the table reading the newspaper.

Liam was playing with some toys instead of eating his breakfast and his mother was pouring herself a cup of coffee. Calum got his breakfast and sat down next to his father.

"Sleep well?" asked his father.

Calum smiled, his mouth was full of cereal.

"Your mom told me you had a dream about dinosaurs," his father continued. "I think you might find this interesting." He handed Calum the newspaper. It was open to the science pages, which was strange because his father never read that section.

Calum took the paper and looked at it. He read the headline out loud "Human and Dinosaur Foot-print Dated 65 Million Years Old!"

"I'm sure it's a mistake," said Calum's father. "I mean we all know it's not possible."

SUNDAY NEWS

Calum continued reading the article. The rock where the footprints were found was fossilized mud. X-rays showed something was buried deep in the rock-hard mud, but it was difficult for scientists to know for sure what it was. The article finished by saying that tests would be performed on the fossil so they could learn what was in the mud. Scientists were certain that whatever it was, it would be able to give them a lot of information about what life was like during the time of the dinosaurs more than 65 million years ago.

Calum smiled. He knew what it was and he wondered what the scientists would do when they learned the mysterious object was an old gym sock.

The End

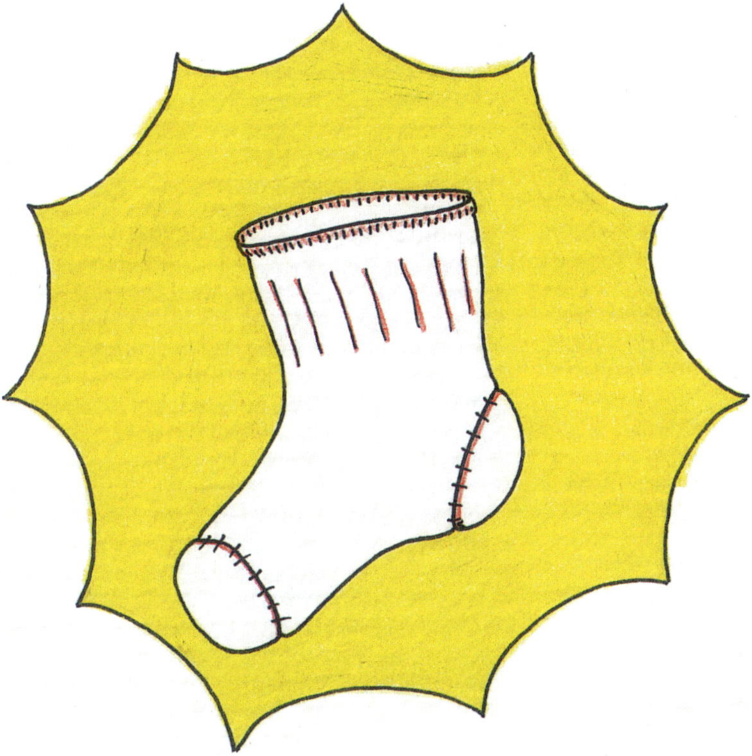

ACTIVITIES

COMPREHENSION QUESTIONS

Read the sentences below. Are they true or false?

	T	F
Calum's magic bed took him to space.		
The huge eggs belonged to a dinosaur.		
Calum liked the taste of the berries that the monkey was eating.		
Calum ran away from a Triceratops and hid in a dark cave.		
There was nothing interesting in the cave.		
Calum found the cat in a tree.		

Now correct the false sentences.

GRAMMAR

Read the sentences below and complete the phrasal verbs with the correct answer.

1. “Mom’s going to be really angry .... me,” he thought.
   ⓐ to ⓑ at ⓒ about
2. But the monkey was only interested .... eating the fruit he found.
   ⓐ on ⓑ for ⓒ in
3. Calum got out .... the bed and started to explore.
   ⓐ by ⓑ from ⓒ of
4. He caught up ...... the monkey and followed it into the cave.
   ⓐ to ⓑ for ⓒ on
5. Calum had been interested .... dinosaurs when he was a little boy.
   ⓐ on ⓑ in ⓒ with

VOCABULARY

Match the words with the correct definitions.

wisdom	the place where a bird lays its eggs
bare	a loud, deep sound
sour	knowledge that is gained by having many experiences in life
thump	not covered by clothing, shoes, a hat, etc.
nest	a part of a tree that grows out from the trunk
branch	having an acid taste

SPEAKING

DINO-QUIZ

Here is a quiz about dinosaurs! Do a little research and try to find the answers. Then you can test your friends and family and see how much they know about dinosaurs. Talk to your friends and tell them what you've learned.

1. Dinosaurs ruled the Earth for ------------------------------------.

(a) 200 years
(b) over 165 million years
(c) about 2 million years

2. The death of all the dinosaurs is believed to be caused by

------------------------------------.

(a) the lions
(b) a bad disease
(c) a massive asteroid impact

3. Dinosaurs lived ------------------------------------.

(a) on all the continents, including Antarctica
(b) only in Africa
(c) on all the continents, except Antarctica

4. A person who studies dinosaurs is known as ________________.

ⓐ a dinosaurist
ⓑ a paleontologist
ⓒ a jurassican

5. Some believe the first dinosaur bones were discovered by the ________________ over 2,000 years ago and they thought they were the bones of giant dragons.

ⓐ Chinese
ⓑ Greeks
ⓒ Mesopotamians

6. Animals that eat meat are called carnivores, animals that eat insects are called insectivores, and animals that eat plants are called ________________.

ⓐ plantivores
ⓑ vegivores
ⓒ herbivores

7. No one knows exactly what color dinosaurs were or what their skin looked like, but scientists think they might have been covered in ________________.

ⓐ fur
ⓑ feathers
ⓒ scales

ANSWERS: 1. b, 2. c, 3. a, 4. b, 5. a, 6. c, 7. b

SOME ANIMALS FROM THE AGE OF DINOSAURS

Edmontonia

Home: North America

Food: plants

Size: 6.5 meters long, 2 meters tall

Cool fact: Its body was protected by an armor.

Maiasaura

Home: North America

Food: plants

Size: 9 meters long, 2.5 meters tall

Cool Fact: Maiasaura means "good mother reptile".

Triceratops

Home: Western North America

Food: plants

Size: 9 meters long, 2 meters tall

Cool Fact: It often acted like a rhinoceros.

- *It is the author's favorite dinosaur!*

Tyrannosaurus rex

Home: North America and East Asia (Mongolia)

Food: meat

Size: 12.4 meters long, 4 meters tall

Cool Fact: It had two clawed fingers.

Morganucodon

Home: China, Europe, North America and South Africa

Food: meat (insects)

Size: 10-15 cm long

Cool Fact: It was a mammal not a dinosaur.

Quetzalcoatlus

Home: North America

Food: meat

Size: 5 meters tall, 11 meters wing span

Cool Fact: It was a reptile not a dinosaur.

WRITING

Which animal is the most interesting for you? Write a paragraph about the animal you choose by using the facts given above. Describe why you find that animal interesting.

GLOSSARY

artwork *(noun)* a painting, sculpture, photograph, etc., that is created to be beautiful or to express an idea or feeling
• The walls were decorated with the **artwork** of a famous artist.

bare *(adjective)* not covered by clothing, shoes, a hat, etc.
• She lost her gloves, so her hands were **bare.**

blind *(verb)* to cause (someone) to be unable to see
• I was **blinded** by the sun after I came out of the cinema.

branch *(noun)* a part of a tree that grows out from the trunk
• She hung a birdhouse to the **branch** of the tree.

caveman *(noun)* a person who lived in a cave in ancient times
• They discovered paintings made by **cavemen** in the Stone Age.

chirp *(verb)* to make a short high-pitched sound
• A blue bird was **chirping** in the tree.

collar *(noun)* a part of a piece of clothing that fits around a person's neck
• The shirt was buttoned all the way up to the **collar.**

come across *(verb)* to meet or find (something or someone) by chance
• As I was walking down the street, I **came across** a cute puppy.

cover *(noun)* a blanket or sheet on a bed
• The little girl was sick, so she lay under the **covers** all day long.

crawl *(verb)* to move on one's hands and knees
• The baby **crawled** before he started to walk.

curl *(verb)* to twist or form (something) into a round or curved shape
• The cat **curled** into a ball and started sleeping at the end of the bed.

groom *(verb)* to clean and care for (an animal)
• A mother cat usually **grooms** its kittens by licking their fur.

growl *(verb)* to make a deep threatening sound
• The dog **growled** at the postman.

hesitate *(verb)* to stop briefly before you do something especially because you are nervous or unsure about what to do
•I didn't know what was behind the door, so I **hesitated** before opening it.

inspect *(verb)* to look at (something) carefully in order to learn more about it, to find problems, etc.
• The detective **inspected** the passport left in the car.

lump *(noun)* a small piece or mass of something
• There was a **lump** of dirty clothes on the floor.

melt *(verb)* to change or to cause (something) to change from a solid to a liquid usually because of heat
• Her ice cream **melted** on this hot summer day.

nest *(noun)* the place where a bird lays its eggs and takes care of its young
• In the **nest** there were three little birds.

pet *(verb)* to touch (a cat, dog, child, etc.) with your hand in a loving or friendly way
• The little boy **petted** the dog in the park.

puddle *(noun)* a small amount of water, mud, etc., on the ground
• It rained all night and now the road was covered in **puddles.**

purr *(verb)* to make or utter a soft vibrant sound
• The cat sat next to me and started **purring.**

runaway *(adjective)* (someone, an animal) who or that has escaped from some place
• They found the **runaway** horse in the empty field.

rustle *(verb)* to make a soft, light sound because parts of something are touching or rubbing against each other
• The leaves of the trees **rustled** in the strong wind.

scoop *(verb)* to pick up (something or someone) in one quick, continuous motion
• The woman **scooped** the baby up from the floor

scratch *(verb)* to rub a surface or object with something sharp or rough in a way that produces a harsh sound
• The tiger **scratched** the tree to sharpen its claws.

scurry *(verb)* to move quickly and with short steps
• The squirrel **scurried** out of the garden.

slurp *(verb)* to eat or drink (something) noisily or with a sucking sound
• The old man **slurped** his soup.

sneak *(verb)* to move quietly and secretly in order to avoid being noticed
• Two boys **sneaked** out of the classroom without their teacher noticing.

sniff *(verb)* to smell by taking short breaths
• She **sniffed** the flowers before putting them into a vase.

snuggle *(verb)* to lie or sit close together in a comfortable position
• The girl **snuggled** to her father and they read a book together.

sour *(adjective)* having an acid taste that is like the taste of a lemon
• He picked an apple from the tree but it was too **sour** to eat.

spit *(verb)* to force (something, such as food or liquid) from your mouth
• I took a bite from the cake but quickly **spit** it out because there was something wrong with its taste.

squeal *(verb)* to make or cause (something) to make a long, high-pitched cry or noise
• I hit the brakes and the car **squealed** to a stop.

sweat *(verb)* to produce a clear liquid from your skin when you are hot or nervous
• It was so hot I started to **sweat** the moment I got out of the house.

swing *(verb)* to move with a smooth, curving motion
• The acrobat was **swinging** from one rope to another.

tap *(verb)* to hit (someone or something) lightly causing a small sound
• She couldn't hear me because of all the noise, so I **tapped** her on the shoulder.

thump *(noun)* a loud, deep sound made especially when a heavy object hits something
• Her suitcase fell to the ground and landed with a **thump.**

treat *(noun)* something that tastes good and that is not eaten often
• Everytime the dog brings the newspaper I give him a **treat** like a cookie dog bone.

tug *(verb)* to pull something with a quick, forceful movement
• He **tugged** on his sweater but no matter how hard he pulled, he couldn't get it over his head.

wisdom *(noun)* knowledge that is gained by having many experiences in life
• She trusted her old teacher's **wisdom** and decided to get advice from him.

SARAH SWEENEY

Sarah was born in 1980 in Halifax, Canada and was raised in a small town called Hubbards. Growing up she spent many hours playing outside and enjoying the fresh air. She traveled a lot with her family, and because of that, she loves to explore. After finishing university, Sarah moved to Istanbul, Turkey, where she lives today with her husband Özgehan and her tailless cat Kuyruk. Sarah is an English teacher and enjoys working with children. In her spare time, Sarah loves doing different crafts, reading and writing, and drawing. She especially loves a good adventure.

Calum is Sarah's nephew, who she doesn't get to see very much, but thinks about all the time. She wishes she had a magic bed so she could visit him more often and go on adventures with him.